# EMOTIONAL SPENDING:

## *WHY YOU BUY WHAT YOU DON'T NEED*

**By Essence Coffey**

Financial Truth Series

**Fire & Inspire Publishing LLC**

# COPYRIGHT PAGE



This publication is intended solely for informational and educational purposes. It does not constitute financial, legal, or professional advice. The author and publisher disclaim any liability for decisions made based on the content herein. Readers are encouraged to consult qualified professionals regarding specific financial circumstances.

The perspectives presented in this work reflect behavioral, psychological, and experiential interpretations of financial decision-making and are designed to support awareness, not replace professional guidance.

Published by: Fire & Inspire Publishing LLC
ISBN: 979-8-90083-504-4
Printed in the United States of America

# DEDICATION

This work is dedicated to the woman who has quietly carried the weight of her own financial contradictions—the one who has resolved, repeatedly, to “do better next month,” while navigating decisions she has not yet fully understood.

Not the version of her that performs stability, but the version that recognizes, with increasing clarity, that something must change.

# AUTHOR'S NOTE

This text is not constructed to comfort denial. It is designed to confront it.

Much of the contemporary discourse surrounding financial behavior is diluted by oversimplification—reduced to prescriptive advice that prioritizes surface-level correction over substantive understanding. Readers are routinely encouraged to "budget better," "exercise discipline," or "increase savings," as though behavioral inconsistency were merely a failure of effort rather than a reflection of deeper psychological patterns.

This work rejects that premise.

Emotional spending is not a peripheral issue. It is a primary behavioral mechanism through which individuals regulate discomfort, avoid confrontation with internal states, and construct temporary relief in the absence of sustainable coping strategies. As such, it cannot be meaningfully addressed through numerical adjustments alone.

What follows is not a collection of motivational statements or temporary interventions. It is an examination—direct at times uncomfortable, but necessary—of the patterns that quietly govern financial behavior.

Readers are not asked to engage with this material passively. They are asked to engage with it honestly.

Not selectively. Not defensively. But with the willingness to observe their own patterns without distortion.

Because without that level of honesty, no system—regardless of its sophistication—will produce lasting change.

# INTRODUCTION

## You Do Not Have a Money Problem—You Have a Pattern

The prevailing assumption that individuals who struggle financially simply lack knowledge or discipline is both widespread and fundamentally flawed. It suggests that access to information is the primary barrier to change. Yet, in practice, individuals often possess more than sufficient exposure to financial principles, budgeting frameworks, savings methodologies, and debt reduction strategies—without demonstrating consistent behavioral alignment.

This discrepancy points to a deeper issue.

Financial behavior is not governed primarily by logic. It is governed by patterns—patterns that are emotional in origin, reinforced through repetition, and sustained through cognitive justification.

Emotional spending is a behavioral adaptation. It emerges not as a deliberate act of irresponsibility, but as a response to internal discomfort. Stress, fatigue, boredom, loneliness, and perceived inadequacy function as catalysts, activating a need for relief that is often satisfied through consumption.

The act of spending, in these instances, serves a purpose beyond acquisition. It provides a temporary shift in emotional state. It offers a sense of control where control feels absent. It introduces stimulation in otherwise stagnant conditions. It creates the illusion of resolution without addressing the underlying cause.

Importantly, this process is neither accidental nor isolated. It is patterned.

Each instance of emotional spending reinforces the association between discomfort and consumption. Over time, this association becomes increasingly automatic, reducing the likelihood of conscious interruption. The behavior transitions from choice to response—from something one does to something one defaults to.

It is for this reason that traditional financial interventions often fail to produce sustained results.

They attempt to correct behavior at the level of decision-making without addressing the mechanisms that drive those decisions. As long as the underlying pattern remains intact, new strategies will be overridden by familiar responses.

The objective of this work is not to impose restriction, nor to advocate for financial perfection. It is to illuminate the pattern.

Because once the pattern is clearly understood, it can be disrupted.

And once it is disrupted, it can be replaced.

That process begins here.

# PART I

## THIS IS NOT ABOUT MONEY

# Chapter 1

## The Misdiagnosis: Why Budgeting Was Never the Problem

The assertion that financial instability is primarily the result of inadequate budgeting persists as one of the most widely accepted yet fundamentally flawed explanations for inconsistent financial behavior. It presents a convenient narrative—one that implies the issue is procedural rather than psychological, suggesting that the application of structure alone is sufficient to produce meaningful change. However, this interpretation fails to account for the persistent discrepancy between knowledge and action that characterizes emotional spending.

Individuals are aware of financial principles. They have engaged with budgeting systems, savings strategies, and debt reduction methods. They have constructed plans, established categories, and, in many cases, demonstrated temporary adherence. Yet, despite this awareness, behavior repeatedly diverges from intention. This divergence is not accidental. It reflects the presence of competing psychological forces that operate beyond the reach of structured financial planning.

In moments of emotional activation—periods marked by stress, fatigue, or internal unrest—the relevance of the budget diminishes. The individual is no longer operating within a long-term framework of discipline and strategy but within an immediate need for relief. In such moments, spending does not present itself as a violation of a plan. It presents itself as a solution.

This distinction is essential. The behavior is not inherently irrational; it is functionally adaptive. It serves a purpose that the budget does not address. Where the budget offer's structure, spending offers emotional regulation. And when these two forces compete, regulation consistently overrides structure.

To continue framing the issue as a failure of budgeting is to address the symptom while ignoring the mechanism. A more accurate inquiry shifts from "Why can I not adhere to a financial plan?" to "What function does this behavior serve when adherence breaks down?" Each deviation from a plan is not merely a lapse; it is data. It reveals the presence of an unmet need—one that is being temporarily resolved through financial behavior.

Until that need is identified and addressed through alternative means, the pattern will persist. Not because the individual lacks discipline, but because the true driver of the behavior remains unexamined.

# Chapter 2

## Emotional Spending Defined: Beyond the Transaction

Emotional spending is frequently misunderstood as impulsive or careless financial behavior. It is neither arbitrary nor devoid of intention. It is a patterned response to internal discomfort, in which financial action is used as a mechanism to alter emotional states. To define it accurately requires a shift away from the transaction itself and toward the psychological process that precedes it.

At its core, emotional spending is not about acquisition. It is about regulation. The individual is not merely purchasing an item; they are seeking relief, stimulation, reassurance, or a sense of control. The object acquired is secondary. The primary outcome is the temporary modification of an internal experience.

This distinction explains why the behavior persists even in the presence of negative consequences. The immediate reward—the shift in emotional state—

outweighs the delayed cost. The brain, conditioned by repeated exposure to this cycle, begins to associate spending with relief. Over time, this association becomes reinforced, creating a predictable pattern: discomfort arises, spending follows, and temporary relief is achieved.

Importantly, this process is often accompanied by cognitive justification. Individuals rarely perceive their behavior as harmful in the moment it occurs. Instead, it is framed through narratives that validate the decision: the belief that the purchase is deserved, minimal, or manageable. These narratives reduce internal resistance, allowing the behavior to proceed without significant psychological conflict.

The challenge, therefore, is not merely behavioral correction. It is cognitive and emotional awareness. Without recognizing the underlying function of the behavior, individuals remain focused on the surface-level act of spending, attempting to correct it through restriction alone. Such efforts are inherently limited, as they do not address the mechanism that sustains the pattern.

To understand emotional spending is to recognize that it is not a failure of financial knowledge. It is a learned response to emotional discomfort—one that must be examined at its source if it is to be effectively changed.

# Chapter 3

## The Critical Moment: The Psychological Space Before Action

Within every instance of emotional spending, there exists a moment that is often overlooked due to its brevity. It is the moment between impulse and action—the point at which the behavior is initiated but not yet completed. Though fleeting, this moment is critical, as it represents the only point within the cycle where interruption is possible.

This moment does not begin with the item. It begins with a shift in internal state. The individual experiences a feeling—subtle or pronounced—that creates a sense of discomfort or restlessness. This may occur in response to external stimuli, such as social comparison or environmental stressors, or it may emerge internally, without a clearly identifiable cause.

Shortly thereafter, an external object is introduced—a product, an opportunity, or a perceived solution. The object is not neutral. It is immediately assigned meaning. It becomes associated with the potential to alleviate the discomfort that preceded it. This association creates a sense of urgency, not necessarily rooted in the object itself, but in the anticipated relief it represents.

At this stage, cognitive processing is limited. The individual is not evaluating long-term consequences or aligning the decision with established goals. Instead, attention is directed toward the immediate outcome—the resolution of discomfort. This shift in focus reduces the influence of prior commitments, allowing the behavior to proceed with minimal resistance.

The speed at which this process occurs contributes to its invisibility. Because the sequence unfolds rapidly, it is rarely examined in real time. The individual becomes aware of the decision only after it has been made, at which point the opportunity for interruption has passed.

However, when this moment is slowed—through intentional observation, it reveals a pattern that is neither random nor uncontrollable. It becomes evident that the behavior is preceded by identifiable cues, both emotional and cognitive. These cues, once recognized, can be used to create space between impulse and action.

It is within this space that agency exists. Not in the elimination of impulse, but in the capacity to respond to it differently. Without awareness of this moment, the behavior remains automatic. With awareness, it becomes subject to choice.

# Chapter 4

## Avoidance as a Behavioral Driver: What You Are Not Addressing

A comprehensive understanding of emotional spending requires an examination of what it replaces. While the behavior presents as an act of acquisition, its function is more accurately described as avoidance. It serves as a diversion from experiences that the individual is either unwilling or unprepared to confront directly.

Avoidance manifests in various forms. It may involve the deferral of problematic decisions, the suppression of emotional discomfort, or the disengagement from realities that feel overwhelming. In each case, the underlying objective is the same: to reduce immediate distress without addressing its source.

Spending provides an effective mechanism for this purpose. It redirects attention, introduces novelty, and creates a sense of forward movement. In doing so, it suspends the need for confrontation. The individual is no longer required to sit with discomfort, as their focus has shifted to the act of consumption.

This redirection is not inherently problematic in isolation. However, when it becomes the primary method of coping, it reinforces a pattern in which discomfort is consistently avoided rather than processed. Over time, this pattern becomes self-sustaining. The individual learns, through repeated experience, that avoidance is effective in the short term, and therefore continues to rely on it.

The consequence of this reliance is not merely financial. It is developmental. By circumventing the need to engage with difficult experiences, the individual limits their capacity to build emotional tolerance. Situations that require sustained attention or reflection are more likely to be avoided, as the individual has not developed alternative strategies for managing discomfort.

Thus, the issue is not simply that money is being spent unnecessarily. It is that spending has become a substitute for engagement. It replaces the processes through which individuals typically develop resilience, clarity, and self-regulation.

To alter this pattern, the focus must shift from the behavior itself to the function it serves. The question is not, “How do I stop spending?” but rather, “What am I avoiding when I choose to spend?” The answer to this question provides the foundation for change. Because once avoidance is identified, it can be addressed directly, reducing the need for substitution.

# Part I Closing Insight

The central premise of this section is both simple and frequently resisted: emotional spending is not a financial problem. It is a behavioral pattern rooted in emotional regulation, cognitive reinforcement, and avoidance.

Efforts to address it at the level of money alone will continue to produce temporary results at best. Sustainable change requires a shift in perspective—from correcting behavior to understanding it. It requires the individual to observe their own patterns without distortion, to recognize the functions those patterns serve, and to develop alternative responses that address the underlying need.

Only then does the possibility of change become not theoretical, but practical.

# PART II

## WHY YOU, DO THIS

# Chapter 5

## Emotional Triggers: The Predictable Origins of Financial Behavior

Emotional spending is often misinterpreted as spontaneous or impulsive; however, closer examination reveals that it is highly predictable. It does not occur in isolation, nor does it arise without cause. It is consistently preceded by identifiable emotional states—triggers that initiate the behavioral sequence leading to financial action.

Among the most prominent of these triggers are stress, loneliness, boredom, insecurity, and social comparison. While these states may differ in origin and intensity, they share a common characteristic: each introduces a form of internal discomfort that the individual seeks to resolve. This discomfort does not demand financial action inherently; rather, financial action has been learned as a reliable means of alleviating it.

Stress, for example, creates a cognitive and physiological burden that reduces the individual's capacity for sustained self-regulation. Under such conditions, the prioritization of long-term goals becomes secondary to immediate relief. Spending, in this context, offers a rapid and accessible form of release—one that requires minimal cognitive effort while producing an immediate emotional shift.

Loneliness operates differently but produces a similar outcome. It reflects a deficit in meaningful connection, which the individual may attempt to compensate for through acquisition. While material goods cannot fulfill relational needs, they can temporarily occupy the psychological space created by their absence, providing distraction rather than resolution.

Boredom introduces yet another pathway. It is not merely the absence of activity but the absence of engagement. In response, the individual seeks stimulation. Modern consumer environments are designed to meet this demand efficiently, offering a continuous stream of options that invite interaction. Spending becomes a form of engagement, replacing inactivity with action.

Insecurity and social comparison further complicate the pattern. When individuals perceive themselves as lacking—whether in status, appearance, or achievement—they may attempt to restore equilibrium through visible markers of adequacy. Consumption, in this sense, becomes symbolic. It is not about the utility of the item, but about what the item represents.

What is critical to understand is that these triggers do not operate randomly. They follow patterns that are consistent within the individual's daily life. Certain times, environments, or contexts increase their likelihood. Without conscious recognition of these patterns, the individual remains reactive responding to triggers as they arise rather than anticipating them.

The identification of triggers, therefore, is not a peripheral exercise. It is foundational. Because until the origin of the behavior is understood, the behavior itself will continue to appear uncontrollable, when it is simply unobserved.

## Chapter 6

## Identity Maintenance: Spending as a Reflection of Self-Concept

Financial behavior cannot be fully understood without considering the role of identity. Individuals do not make decisions in a vacuum; they make decisions in alignment with how they perceive themselves, or how they wish to be perceived. Spending, in this context, becomes a tool not only for emotional regulation but for identity maintenance.

The statements that often accompany emotional spending—“I deserve this,” “I’ve been through enough,” or “I need to look like I’m doing well”—are not merely justifications. They are expressions of an underlying self-concept. They reveal the narratives individuals hold about themselves and the ways in which they attempt to preserve or reinforce those narratives through behavior.

The concept of deservingness, for instance, is frequently invoked as a rationale for spending. While it may originate from legitimate experiences of hardship or effort, it can become distorted when used to override boundaries. The individual is no longer evaluating the purchase based on necessity or alignment with long-term goals, but on its capacity to affirm a sense of self-worth.

Similarly, the desire to appear stable or successful introduces a performative element into financial behavior. The individual is not only responding to internal states but also to perceived external expectations. Spending becomes a means of signaling adequacy, even when it does not reflect actual stability. This dissonance between appearance and reality creates additional pressure, which may, in turn, perpetuate further spending.

What complicates this dynamic is that identity is inherently resistant to change. When behavior is tied to self-concept, altering that behavior requires more than surface-level adjustment. It requires a re-evaluation of the narratives that support it. Without such re-evaluation, attempts to change spending habits may feel threatening, as though the individual is not merely adjusting a behavior but compromising their identity.

Thus, the persistence of emotional spending is not solely a matter of habit. It is a matter of alignment. Individuals continue to engage in behaviors that reinforce who they believe themselves to be, even when those behaviors produce undesirable outcomes.

To disrupt this pattern, identity must be separated from behavior. The individual must come to understand that their worth, stability, and adequacy are not contingent upon what they acquire. Only then can financial decisions be made from a place of clarity rather than self-preservation.

# Chapter 7

## Developmental Conditioning: The Origins of Financial Behavior

Financial behavior does not emerge in isolation during adulthood. It is shaped, often unconsciously, by early experiences and environmental conditioning. The ways in which individuals perceive, interact with, and respond to money are influenced by the contexts in which those patterns were first observed and reinforced.

For some, early experiences of scarcity create a sense of urgency around money. When resources were limited or unpredictable, the act of spending upon acquisition becomes a learned response. The underlying belief—often unarticulated—is that money is temporary and must be used before it disappears. This belief persists even when circumstances change, leading to behaviors that are misaligned with current reality.

For others, the absence of financial dialogue during formative years results in a lack of structured understanding. Money was present but unexamined, used but not discussed. In such cases, individuals enter adulthood without a framework for intentional financial behavior. They rely instead on reactive patterns, making decisions in response to immediate circumstances rather than guided by established principles.

Additionally, modeled behavior plays a significant role. Individuals who observed emotional spending in caregivers or significant others may internalize these patterns without conscious awareness. Shopping as a response to stress, reward, or disappointment becomes normalized, not as a deliberate choice, but as an inherited behavior.

In some instances, periods of deprivation, whether financial or experiential, lead to compensatory behavior later in life. Access to resources, once limited, is now perceived as an opportunity to reclaim what was previously unavailable. While this may initially feel like freedom, it can evolve into a lack of restraint if not accompanied by intentional regulation.

What unites these varied experiences is the concept of conditioning. Financial behaviors are learned responses, shaped by repeated exposure to specific environments and reinforced through outcomes. They are not arbitrary, nor are they fixed. However, without conscious examination, they continue to operate as default patterns.

Understanding the origins of these behaviors does not serve to assign blame, but to provide context. It allows the individual to recognize that their current patterns are not inherent traits but acquired responses. And what has been acquired can, with intention, be modified.

# Chapter 8

## Neurochemical Reinforcement: The Dopamine-Driven Cycle

While emotional and cognitive factors play a significant role in spending behavior, they are further reinforced by neurobiological processes that increase the likelihood of repetition. Central to this reinforcement is dopamine, a neurotransmitter associated with reward, motivation, and reinforcement learning.

Dopamine is not released solely upon receiving a reward; it is released in anticipation of it. This distinction is critical in understanding emotional spending. The act of browsing, selecting, and purchasing activates the brain's reward system even before the item is acquired. The anticipation itself becomes a source of pleasure.

This mechanism explains why the process of spending often feels more satisfying than the outcome. The excitement of adding items to a cart, completing a transaction, or awaiting delivery generates a sustained sense of anticipation. Once the item is received, the emotional impact frequently diminishes, as the anticipatory phase has concluded.

Over time, the brain learns to associate spending with this reward cycle. The sequence—anticipation, action, reward—is encoded as a reliable pathway for achieving positive emotional states. When discomfort arises, the brain retrieves this pathway as a solution, prompting the individual to engage in the same behavior.

This process operates outside conscious awareness. It does not require deliberate decision-making; it is triggered automatically in response to familiar cues. As a result, individuals may find themselves engaging in spending behavior even when they intellectually recognize its negative consequences.

The presence of this neurochemical reinforcement does not eliminate the possibility of change, but it does complicate it. It requires the individual to work against a system that has been conditioned to prioritize immediate reward over long-term outcomes.

To disrupt this cycle, alternative sources of reward must be established ones that do not carry the same negative consequences. This does not occur instantaneously. It requires repetition, consistency, and the gradual reconditioning of the brain's response to discomfort.

Understanding the role of dopamine reframes the issue. It shifts the narrative from one of personal failure to one of conditioned response. The individual is not lacking discipline; they are responding to a system that has been trained to seek relief through specific behaviors.

## Part II Closing Insight

The persistence of emotional spending cannot be adequately explained through surface-level analysis. It is the result of an intricate interplay between emotional triggers, identity maintenance, developmental conditioning, and neurochemical reinforcement. Each of these elements contributes to the formation and continuation of the pattern.

Attempts to change behavior without addressing these underlying mechanisms are inherently limited. They focus on the visible outcome while ignoring the processes that produce it. As a result, they yield temporary compliance rather than sustained transformation.

True change requires a comprehensive understanding of the system. It requires the individual to recognize not only what they are doing, but why they are doing it, how it has been reinforced, and what it has come to represent.

Only with this level of understanding can the pattern be effectively disrupted.

Because once the system is understood, it is no longer invisible.

And what is no longer invisible can no longer operate unchecked.

# PART III

# HOW IT MANIFESTS IN REAL LIFE

## Chapter 9

# Compensatory Reward Cycles: "I Deserve This" as Behavioral Justification

Among the most socially accepted forms of emotional spending is the compensatory reward cycle, commonly framed through the language of deservingness. The individual, having experienced exertion, stress, or perceived deprivation, engages in spending as a form of self-reward. On the surface, this behavior appears rational—an earned response to effort. However, upon closer examination, it reveals a substitution of genuine restoration with consumptive relief.

The underlying premise of this cycle is not inherently flawed. The recognition that effort warrants recovery is valid. The issue arises in the method of recovery employed. Rather than engaging in restorative practices that address the source of depletion—such as rest, reflection, or boundary-setting—the individual defaults to acquisition. The purchase becomes a proxy for recovery, offering immediacy where true restoration requires time and intentionality.

This substitution is reinforced by the immediacy of its effects. Spending produces a rapid emotional shift, creating the perception that relief has been achieved. However, this relief is transient. It does not resolve the underlying exhaustion or stress that prompted the behavior. Consequently, the individual remains depleted, necessitating repeated engagement in the same cycle.

Over time, this pattern becomes self-perpetuating. Work or stress leads to spending; spending provides temporary relief but does not restore capacity; diminished capacity leads to further stress, which in turn justifies additional spending. The cycle continues, not because it is effective, but because it is immediate.

What makes this pattern particularly resistant to change is its perceived legitimacy. Because the behavior is framed as a reward, it is rarely questioned. The individual does not interpret it as problematic, but as justified. This framing reduces the likelihood of critical evaluation, allowing the cycle to persist without interruption.

To disrupt this pattern, the concept of reward must be redefined. True reward must be distinguished from temporary relief. It must contribute to restoration rather than merely distraction. Without this distinction, the cycle will continue to operate under the guise of self-care while producing the opposite effect.

# Chapter 10

## Comparative Distortion: The Psychological Impact of Social Referencing

The role of social comparison in shaping financial behavior is both subtle and profound. Individuals do not evaluate their circumstances in isolation; they do so relative to the perceived status of others. This process, known as comparative referencing, becomes particularly influential in environments saturated with curated representations of success and stability.

The distortion arises not from the existence of comparison itself, but from its interpretation. Observations of others' achievements, lifestyles, or possessions are often internalized as indicators of personal deficiency. The individual does not merely acknowledge difference; they assign meaning to it. The presence of perceived disparity becomes evidence of inadequacy.

This interpretation generates discomfort—an internal tension between current reality and perceived expectation. In response, the individual seeks to reduce this tension. Ideally, this would occur through constructive action, such as skill development or long-term planning. However, such approaches require time and sustained effort. In contrast, spending offers an immediate, though superficial, means of narrowing the perceived gap.

Consumption, in this context, functions symbolically. It does not alter the underlying disparity, but it creates the appearance of alignment. The individual acquires or adopts behaviors that signal proximity to the desired standard, thereby reducing immediate discomfort. However, because the underlying comparison remains unresolved, the relief is temporary.

What complicates this dynamic is the absence of a fixed endpoint. Social comparison is inherently open-ended. There will always exist individuals who appear to possess more, achieve more, or progress more rapidly. As such, attempts to resolve comparative discomfort through spending are inherently unsustainable. The target continually shifts, rendering satisfaction perpetually out of reach.

The consequence is a cycle in which the individual remains in a state of perceived insufficiency, responding to each iteration through consumption. This not only perpetuates financial instability but also reinforces the belief that self-worth is externally determined.

Breaking this cycle requires a fundamental shift in evaluative framework. The individual must transition from external referencing to internal assessment—measuring progress against personal values and objectives rather than perceived social benchmarks. Without this shift, comparison will continue to function as a trigger, and spending will remain its default response.

# Chapter 11

## Concealment and Fragmentation: The Dynamics of Secret Spending

As emotional spending patterns intensify, they often give rise to a secondary behavior: concealment. The individual, aware at some level of the misalignment between their actions and their intentions, begins to obscure or minimize the extent of their financial behavior. This concealment may be directed toward others, such as partners or family members, or toward oneself, through avoidance of financial review and selective attention.

This phenomenon extends beyond mere omission. It represents a fragmentation of the self. The individual maintains parallel narratives: one aligned with responsibility and intention, and another characterized by exception and contradiction. These narratives coexist without integration, creating internal dissonance.

The psychological cost of this fragmentation is significant. It erodes self-trust, as the individual becomes aware of their own inconsistency. Commitments lose credibility, both internally and externally. The individual may continue to articulate goals and intentions, but their belief in their capacity to uphold them diminishes.

In relational contexts, concealment introduces additional complexity. Financial behavior, when hidden, undermines transparency and trust. Even in the absence of explicit discovery, the act of concealment creates psychological distance. The individual is no longer fully present within the relationship, as a portion of their behavior exists outside of shared awareness.

Importantly, concealment is not the origin of the problem; it is a response to it. It emerges as a mechanism to manage the discomfort associated with misalignment. By avoiding full acknowledgment, the individual temporarily reduces the emotional impact of their behavior. However, this reduction is achieved at the cost of clarity.

Without clarity, change is not possible. The behavior remains unexamined, the pattern unaddressed. Concealment, therefore, functions as both a symptom and a barrier—evidence of the underlying issue and an obstacle to its resolution.

The restoration of integrity requires the reintegration of these fragmented narratives. The individual must be willing to observe their behavior without minimization, to reconcile intention with action, and to reestablish alignment. This process is not immediate, but it is essential. Without it, the pattern will continue to operate beneath the surface, unchallenged.

# Chapter 12

# Aspirational Consumption: Purchasing an Imagined Identity

A particularly compelling manifestation of emotional spending is aspirational consumption—the acquisition of goods or services associated with a desired future self. Unlike reactive spending, which responds to immediate emotional triggers, aspirational spending is oriented toward transformation. It is driven by the belief that external acquisition can facilitate internal change.

This belief is not entirely unfounded. Environmental cues and tools can support behavioral shifts. However, aspirational consumption becomes problematic when it substitutes for the processes required to achieve the desired identity. The individual invests in the symbols of change without engaging in the behaviors that sustain it.

The appeal of this pattern lies in its optimism. It is framed not as indulgence, but as investment. The purchase represents a commitment to a new standard declaration of intent. In the moment of acquisition, the individual experiences a sense of progress, as though the transformation has already begun.

However, this sense of progress is often illusory. Without corresponding behavioral change, the purchased items remain underutilized or abandoned. The individual returns to existing patterns, now accompanied by additional possessions that serve as reminders of unrealized intention.

Over time, this cycle can produce a form of cognitive fatigue. The individual becomes wary of their own declarations of change, having repeatedly failed to sustain them. This skepticism further undermines self-trust, reinforcing the perception that transformation is unattainable.

The resolution of this pattern requires a reversal of sequence. Rather than acquiring in anticipation of change, the individual must initiate change through behavior. Acquisition, if it occurs, should follow demonstrated consistency, serving to support rather than substitute for transformation.

Only then can aspirational elements function as reinforcement rather than distraction.

# Chapter 13

## Material Accumulation and Psychological Residue: The Weight of Unused Acquisition

The consequences of emotional spending extend beyond financial metrics into the physical and psychological environment of the individual. Accumulated items—often unused, underutilized, or forgotten—serve as tangible evidence of prior decisions. These objects are not neutral; they carry associative meaning.

Each item represents a moment in which a narrative was constructed and acted upon. The belief that the purchase would provide relief, facilitate change, or resolve discomfort is embedded within the object itself. When the anticipated outcome fails to materialize, the object becomes a marker of that discrepancy.

This accumulation produces a form of psychological residue. The individual, upon encountering these items, is reminded—consciously or unconsciously—of the misalignment between expectation and outcome. This can evoke feelings of guilt, frustration, or regret. In response, the individual may avoid engaging with these items altogether, further reinforcing avoidance patterns.

The environment, therefore, becomes an extension of the internal state. Clutter is not merely disorganization; it is the physical manifestation of unresolved decisions. It reflects a history of attempts to address internal experiences through external means.

This dynamic has implications for future behavior. The presence of accumulated items can contribute to cognitive overload, reducing the individual's capacity for clear decision-making. It can also normalize excess, making additional acquisition appear less consequential.

Addressing this aspect of emotional spending requires more than organizational strategies. It requires a re-evaluation of the relationship between acquisition and meaning. The individual must recognize that objects do not resolve internal states. Without this recognition, accumulation will continue, regardless of attempts to manage its effects.

## Part III Closing Insight

Emotional spending does not exist as an abstract concept; it manifests in consistent, observable patterns within daily life. These patterns—compensatory reward cycles, comparative distortion, concealment, aspirational consumption, and material accumulation—represent different expressions of the same underlying mechanism.

Each pattern serves a function. Each provides temporary resolution to an internal experience. And each, in its own way, reinforces the continuation of the behavior.

Understanding these manifestations is critical. It allows the individual to move beyond general awareness and into specific recognition. Patterns that were once perceived as isolated or situational become identifiable as part of a broader system.

Once identified, these patterns can no longer operate with the same degree of invisibility. And without invisibility, their influence begins to diminish.

It is at this point—when behavior is no longer unconscious—that the possibility of deliberate change emerges.

# PART IV

# THE COST: WHAT THIS PATTERN IS ACTUALLY DOING

## Chapter 14

# Financial Erosion: Visible Losses and Invisible Trade-Offs

The most immediately recognizable consequence of emotional spending is financial in nature. It is reflected in account balances, credit utilization, recurring debt cycles, and the persistent inability to sustain savings. These outcomes are observable, measurable, and often serve as the primary indicator that a problem exists. However, focusing exclusively on these visible losses is to overlook a more significant dimension of financial erosion: the cumulative effect of foregone opportunities.

Every financial decision represents an allocation of resources, and by extension, a trade-off. When resources are directed toward short-term emotional relief, they are simultaneously removed from potential long-term utility. This includes not only traditional investments, such as savings and asset-building, but also opportunities for flexibility, security, and strategic decision-making.

The concept of opportunity cost is critical in this context. Emotional spending does not merely reduce current financial standing; it constrains future options. The individual may find themselves unable to respond effectively to unexpected expenses, pursue desired opportunities, or transition into more stable circumstances—not because these options are inherently unattainable, but because the resources required to access them have been incrementally depleted.

What distinguishes emotional spending from isolated financial missteps is its repetitive nature. Individual transactions may appear insignificant when evaluated independently. However, their cumulative impact is substantial. Small, consistent deviations from intentional spending compound over time, creating financial conditions that appear disproportionate to any single decision.

Additionally, the delayed nature of financial consequences contributes to their persistence. The immediate effect of spending is relief, while the cost is deferred. This temporal separation weakens the perceived connection between action and outcome, allowing the behavior to continue without immediate correction.

Thus, the financial cost of emotional spending is not limited to what is spent. It encompasses what is no longer available, what has been postponed, and what may no longer be accessible because of repeated short-term prioritization. Without recognition of these broader implications, the behavior is likely to persist, as its full impact remains obscured.

# Chapter 15

## Psychological Consequences: Guilt, Cognitive Dissonance, and Shame Formation

Beyond financial implications, emotional spending exerts a significant psychological impact. These effects are less visible but often more enduring, influencing not only behavior but also self-perception. The immediate aftermath of emotional spending frequently includes a shift in emotional state—from relief to discomfort—as the individual becomes aware of the discrepancy between intention and action.

This discrepancy produces cognitive dissonance, a state in which conflicting beliefs and behaviors coexist. The individual may simultaneously view themselves as responsible and capable while engaging in behavior that contradicts this identity. The resulting tension necessitates resolution, which is often achieved through rationalization or minimization rather than behavioral change.

Over time, repeated experiences of dissonance contribute to the development of guilt. Unlike immediate emotional discomfort, guilt is reflective. It involves an evaluation of one's actions against internal standards. When these evaluations consistently yield negative conclusions, the emotional response intensifies, transitioning from situational guilt to a more generalized sense of inadequacy.

If this pattern continues without resolution, guilt may evolve into shame. While guilt is associated with specific actions, shame is associated with identity. The individual no longer perceives the behavior as inconsistent with who they are; they begin to perceive it as indicative of who they are. This shift has profound implications for behavior, as identity-based beliefs are more resistant to change than situational evaluations.

Shame introduces a paradox. While it creates discomfort that might otherwise motivate change, it also promotes avoidance. The individual, seeking to escape the negative self-perception, may engage in further emotional spending as a coping mechanism.

In this way, the psychological consequences of the behavior become contributors to its continuation.

The recognition of this progression—from dissonance to guilt to shame—is essential. It highlights the importance of early intervention at the level of awareness and cognitive evaluation. Without such intervention, the psychological cost of emotional spending extends beyond isolated experiences, shaping the individual's broader sense of self.

## Chapter 16

## Identity Degradation: The Internalization of Behavioral Patterns

As emotional spending persists, its influence extends into the domain of identity formation. Repeated behaviors, particularly those that contradict stated intentions, contribute to the development of self-perception. The individual begins to interpret their actions not as isolated events, but as evidence of enduring traits.

This process of internalization is subtle but consequential. Statements such as “I struggle with money” or “I lack discipline” may initially function as observations. However, when reinforced through repeated experience, they evolve into identity-based beliefs. The individual no longer views the behavior as something they do; they view it as something they are.

Identity-based beliefs exert a powerful influence on future behavior. They shape expectations, inform decision-making, and determine the range of perceived possibilities. When individuals identify as lacking control or consistency, they are less likely to engage in behaviors that require these qualities. This creates a self-reinforcing cycle in which belief and behavior continuously validate one another.

The degradation of identity in this context is not the result of a single event, but of cumulative experience. Each instance of misalignment contributes incrementally, reinforcing the belief that change is unlikely or unattainable. Over time, this belief becomes self-limiting, reducing the individual's willingness to attempt meaningful change.

It is important to note that this process is not indicative of inherent incapacity. It reflects the natural tendency of the mind to construct coherent narratives based on observed patterns. When the observed pattern is one of inconsistency, the resulting narrative reflects that inconsistency.

Interrupting this process requires the introduction of new evidence—behaviors that contradict the existing narrative. However, this is difficult to achieve when the individual's belief system does not support the possibility of such behavior. Thus, identity degradation functions as both a consequence of emotional spending and a barrier to its resolution.

# Chapter 17

## Erosion of Self-Trust: The Breakdown of Internal Credibility

One of the most significant, yet often overlooked, consequences of emotional spending is the erosion of self-trust. Self-trust refers to the individual's confidence in their ability to follow through on intentions, uphold commitments, and act in alignment with their stated values. It is foundational to effective decision-making and sustained behavioral change.

Emotional spending undermines self-trust through repeated cycles of intention and contradiction. The individual sets a plan or establishes a boundary, only to override it in moments of emotional activation. Each instance of override weakens the credibility of future commitments. Over time, the individual begins to anticipate their own inconsistency.

This anticipation has practical implications. When individuals do not trust themselves to follow through, they are less likely to invest in long-term planning.

Goals are perceived as temporary strategies as unreliable. The individual may continue to articulate intentions, but their belief in the likelihood of success diminishes.

The erosion of self-trust also affects the individual's response to setbacks. Without a foundation of credibility, deviations from intended behavior are interpreted as confirmation of failure rather than opportunities for adjustment. This interpretation discourages persistence, increasing the likelihood of disengagement.

Importantly, self-trust is not restored through intention alone. It is rebuilt through consistent action. Small, reliable behaviors that align with stated commitments gradually reestablish credibility. However, this process requires the individual to engage in behavior that contradicts their current expectations task that becomes more difficult as self-trust declines.

Thus, the erosion of self-trust represents a critical juncture. It is both a consequence of emotional spending and a determinant of future behavior. Without addressing it, efforts to change financial habits are likely to be undermined by a lack of internal confidence.

# Chapter 18

## Delayed Consequences: The Illusion of Harmless Behavior

A defining characteristic of emotional spending is the temporal separation between action and consequence. The immediate outcome of spending is a positive reduction in discomfort, an increase in perceived control, or a momentary sense of satisfaction. The negative consequences, by contrast, are delayed. They emerge over time, often in aggregate rather than in response to a single decision.

This delay creates an illusion of harmlessness. Individual transactions appear inconsequential, as their immediate impact is minimal. The absence of immediate negative feedback reduces the likelihood of behavioral correction. The individual does not experience a direct, immediate cost, and therefore has little incentive to alter their behavior in the moment.

However, delayed consequences do not equate to diminished consequences. They accumulate. Each decision contributes incrementally to a larger outcome that becomes visible only after repeated occurrences. By the time the cumulative effect is recognized, the pattern is often well established.

This dynamic is further complicated by attribution. When consequences finally emerge, they may not be directly associated with the behaviors that produced them. The individual may attribute financial strain to external factors rather than to the accumulation of prior decisions. This misattribution prevents accurate evaluation and perpetuates the cycle.

The illusion of harmlessness is thus sustained by two factors: the delay of consequences and the fragmentation of cause and effect. To disrupt this illusion, the individual must develop the capacity to evaluate decisions not only based on immediate outcomes, but on their cumulative impact.

This requires a shift in temporal perspective—from short-term relief to long-term alignment. Without this shift, the pattern of emotional spending will continue to operate under the perception that its effects are minimal, when they are substantial.

# Part IV Closing Insight

The cost of emotional spending extends far beyond monetary loss. It encompasses psychological strain, identity distortion, and the erosion of self-trust. These effects are interconnected, each reinforcing the others in a system that perpetuates the behavior.

What makes this system particularly resilient is its structure. Immediate rewards mask delayed consequences. Cognitive justifications reduce resistance. Identity-based beliefs limit the perceived possibility of change. Together, these elements create a pattern that is both self-sustaining and difficult to interrupt.

Understanding the full scope of these costs is essential. It shifts the perception of emotional spending from a series of isolated decisions to a comprehensive behavioral system with far-reaching implications.

And once the system is understood in its entirety, the rationale for change becomes not only clear, but necessary.

# PART V

## THE RESET: RESTRUCTURING BEHAVIOR THROUGH AWARENESS AND SYSTEMS

# Chapter 19

## Awareness as the Precondition for Control

Behavioral change cannot occur in the absence of awareness. While this principle is widely acknowledged, it is often misunderstood in practice. Awareness is not merely the recognition that a problem exists; it is the detailed observation of how that problem manifests in real time. It requires the individual to move beyond generalized statements—such as "I spend too much"—and into precise identification of patterns.

Emotional spending, as established in prior sections, is not random. It follows a sequence: emotional activation, cognitive justification, behavioral response, and subsequent consequence. However, this sequence typically unfolds without conscious observation. The individual experiences the outcome without fully registering the process that produced it.

To establish control, this process must be made visible.

This involves examining not only when spending occurs, but the conditions under which it becomes most likely. What emotional states precede it? What environmental cues are present? What internal narratives are activated in the moments leading up to the decision? These questions are not rhetorical; they are diagnostic. They transform behavior from something that "happens" into something that can be studied.

Importantly, awareness must be observational rather than evaluative. Judgment introduces distortion. When individuals approach their behavior with criticism, they are more likely to conceal or minimize it, thereby reducing the accuracy of their observations. In contrast, a neutral stance allows for clearer recognition of patterns.

This distinction is critical. Awareness is not intended to produce immediate correction. Its function is to generate data. The individual becomes a participant-observer in their own behavior, identifying recurring sequences without attempting to interrupt them prematurely.

Over time, this accumulation of data reveals consistency. Patterns previously considered situational have become increasingly predictable. The individual begins to anticipate triggers, recognize justifications, and identify the moments in which deviation from intention is most likely to occur.

It is at this point that control becomes possible.

Not because the behavior has been forcibly suppressed, but because it is no longer invisible. And behavior that is no longer invisible cannot operate with the same degree of automaticity.

# Chapter 20

## Interrupting Automaticity: The Function of Deliberate Pause

Once awareness has been established, the next objective is interruption. Emotional spending persists largely because it operates automatically. The sequence from impulse to action is rapid, leaving little opportunity for conscious intervention. To alter this pattern, a mechanism must be introduced that slows the process sufficiently to allow for alternative responses.

This mechanism is the deliberate pause.

The pause is not an act of refusal; it is an act of delay. Its purpose is not to eliminate the desire to spend, but to create temporal space between impulse and action. Within this space, the individual is afforded the opportunity to engage in reflective evaluation rather than reactive behavior.

The effectiveness of the pause lies in its simplicity. Rather than requiring complex decision-making, it introduces a single condition: no unplanned action occurs immediately. This condition disrupts the urgency that characterizes emotional spending, reducing the intensity of the impulse.

During this pause, the individual engages with a structured set of inquiries: What emotional state is present? What event preceded this impulse? What outcome is being sought through this action? These questions are not intended to produce definitive answers in every instance, but to redirect attention from the object of desire to the process that generated it.

The introduction of this reflective process has a measurable effect. It shifts the individual from a reactive state to a deliberate one. The impulse, while still present, is no longer the sole determinant of behavior. It becomes one factor among several, subject to evaluation rather than immediate execution.

Initially, the pause may produce discomfort. This discomfort is not indicative of failure; it is evidence of interruption. The individual is resisting a familiar pattern, and the absence of immediate relief creates tension. However, this tension diminishes with repetition, as the brain adapts to the new sequence.

Over time, the pause becomes integrated into the behavioral pattern itself. What was once automatic now includes a moment of consideration. This modification, though seemingly minor, represents a fundamental shift—from compulsion to choice.

# Chapter 21

## Behavioral Substitution: Replacing Function, Not Just Form

A common error in attempts to reduce emotional spending is the exclusive focus on elimination. Individuals seek to stop the behavior without addressing the function it serves. As a result, they are left without an alternative means of managing the emotional states that prompted the behavior, increasing the likelihood of relapsing.

Effective change requires substitution.

Substitution, in this context, does not involve replacing spending with arbitrary activity. It involves identifying behaviors that fulfill the same functional role without producing the same negative consequences. If spending serves as a mechanism for stress reduction, the substitute must address stress. If it provides stimulation in response to boredom, the substitute must offer engagement.

This functional approach distinguishes substitution from distraction. Distraction temporarily shifts attention without addressing the underlying state. Substitution, by contrast, engages with the state directly. It provides a means of regulation that is sustainable and aligned with long-term objectives.

The identification of effective substitutes requires experimentation. Individuals must assess which activities produce a measurable shift in their emotional state. These activities may vary significantly depending on the individual, but their defining characteristic is their capacity to address the need that spending previously fulfilled.

It is important to note that substitutes may not replicate the immediacy or intensity of the reward associated with spending. This discrepancy is a function of the neurochemical reinforcement discussed previously. However, with consistent use, alternative behaviors can establish their own patterns of reinforcement, gradually reducing reliance on spending.

The objective is not to eliminate desire, but to redirect response. By providing the individual with viable alternatives, the system of emotional regulation is expanded. Spending is no longer the sole available mechanism, reducing its dominance within the behavioral pattern.

# Chapter 22

## Structural Boundaries: Reducing Decision Fatigue Through Pre-Commitment

While awareness and substitution address the internal components of emotional spending, structural boundaries address their external conditions. These boundaries function as pre-commitments—decisions made in advance that limit the range of available actions in moments of emotional activation.

The necessity of such boundaries arises from the limitations of decision-making under stress. When individuals are emotionally activated, their capacity for complex evaluation is reduced. Reliance on in-the-moment decision-making in such conditions is therefore unreliable. Pre-commitment mitigates this limitation by transferring decision-making to a context in which the individual is not under emotional strain.

Effective boundaries are characterized by clarity and specificity. Vague intentions—such as "spend less" or "be more disciplined"—provide insufficient guidance in moments of decision. In contrast, defined parameters—such as predetermined spending limits, waiting periods for non-essential purchases, or restrictions on specific categories—reduce ambiguity and simplify choices.

These boundaries serve as a protective function. They do not restrict the individual arbitrarily; they safeguard against predictable deviations. By limiting the conditions under which spending can occur, they reduce the likelihood of reactive behavior.

Importantly, boundaries must be realistic. Overly restrictive conditions are unlikely to be maintained and may lead to cycles of adherence and abandonment. The objective is not perfection, but consistency. Boundaries should be designed to be sustainable, allowing for flexibility within a structured framework.

Over time, adherence to these boundaries contributes to the development of discipline. Not as an abstract concept, but as a practiced behavior. The individual becomes accustomed to operating within defined parameters, reducing the cognitive effort required to maintain alignment.

In this way, structural boundaries complement internal awareness. Together, they create a system in which both internal and external factors are addressed, increasing the likelihood of sustained change.

# Chapter 23

## Decoupling Identity from Behavior: Reconstructing Self-Concept

As previously established, emotional spending is often intertwined with identity. It functions not only as a response to emotional states but as a means of maintaining or projecting a particular self-concept. This connection complicates efforts to change behavior, as modifications may be perceived as threats to identity.

To achieve sustainable change, this association must be dismantled.

The individual must recognize that behavior does not define identity. While repeated behaviors contribute to self-perception, they are not immutable indicators of character. They are patterns—acquired, reinforced, and, therefore, capable of modification.

Decoupling identity from behavior involves a shift in narrative. Instead of interpreting spending patterns as evidence of inherent traits, the individual reframes them as learned responses. This reframing reduces the emotional weight associated with change. The individual is no longer attempting to alter who they are, but how they respond.

This distinction is critical. When identity remains tied to behavior, efforts to change may be resisted at a subconscious level. The behavior, despite its negative consequences, provides continuity. It reinforces a known self-concept. Altering it introduces uncertainty, which may be perceived as destabilizing.

By separating identity from behavior, the individual creates space for experimentation. New patterns can be adopted without threatening the core sense of self. Over time, as these patterns are reinforced, they contribute to the development of a revised self-concept—one that reflects alignment rather than contradiction.

This process is gradual. Identity does not shift instantaneously; it evolves through consistent evidence. Each instance of aligned behavior contributes to this evolution, gradually replacing prior narratives with new ones.

# Chapter 24

## Incremental Reinforcement: Rebuilding Control Through Consistency

The restoration of control is not achieved through singular, transformative actions. It is the result of repeated, incremental behaviors that align with intended outcomes. This process, known as incremental reinforcement, emphasizes consistency over magnitude.

Emotional spending often creates the expectation that change must be equally dramatic. Individuals may attempt to make comprehensive overhauls of their financial behavior, implementing extensive restrictions or adopting complex systems. While these efforts may produce short-term results, they are frequently unsustainable.

In contrast, incremental reinforcement focuses on small, repeatable actions. Each instance of adherence—whether it involves pausing before a purchase, selecting an alternative behavior, or maintaining a predefined boundary—serves as evidence of capability. These instances accumulate, gradually altering both behavior and self-perception.

The significance of these small actions lies in their frequency. While individual instances may appear insignificant, their repetition creates a pattern. This pattern, once established, begins to function automatically, reducing the effort required to maintain it.

Additionally, incremental reinforcement contributes to the restoration of self-trust. As the individual observes consistent alignment between intention and action, their confidence in their ability to follow through increases. This confidence, in turn, supports further adherence, creating a positive feedback loop.

It is important to emphasize that this process does not require perfection. Occasional deviations do not negate progress. What matters is the overall trajectory, the extent to which aligned behaviors are repeated over time.

Through this approach, control is not imposed; it is developed. It emerges as a byproduct of consistent action, rather than as a prerequisite for it.

## Part V Closing Insight

The process of change is not achieved through isolated strategies, but through the integration of awareness, interruption, substitution, structure, and identity reconstruction. Each component addresses a different aspect of the behavioral system, contributing to a comprehensive approach.

Emotional spending persists because it fulfills multiple functions—emotional, cognitive, and behavioral. To reduce its influence, these functions must be addressed collectively. Partial interventions may produce temporary improvement, but sustained change requires systemic adjustment.

Part V represents this adjustment. It provides a framework through which the individual can transition from reactive behavior to deliberate action. It does not eliminate emotional responses, nor does it require their suppression. Instead, it introduces alternative pathways that align with long-term objectives.

Through consistent application, these pathways become the new pattern.

And once a new pattern is established, the previous one loses its dominance—not through force, but through replacement.

# PART VI

## BECOMING A WOMAN WHO DOES NOT NEED TO ESCAPE

# Chapter 25

## Emotional Discipline: The Capacity to Feel Without Reacting

At the foundation of sustained behavioral change lies emotional discipline construct frequently misunderstood as suppression, when in fact it represents regulation. Emotional discipline does not require the elimination of discomfort; it requires the ability to experience discomfort without engaging in automatic behavioral responses.

Emotional spending, as previously established, is fundamentally reactive. It is a behavior initiated not by deliberation, but by the immediate need to alter an internal state. The individual experiences discomfort and responds through consumption, effectively bypassing the processes required to engage with that discomfort directly.

Emotional discipline interrupts this sequence.

It introduces a capacity that is both simple in concept and complex in execution: the ability to remain present with an emotional experience without attempting to escape it. This capacity is not innate; it is developed through repeated exposure and intentional practice. The individual learns to tolerate discomfort, to observe it without immediate resolution, and to allow it to exist without assigning its behavioral consequence.

This process is critical because it addresses the root of the pattern. If discomfort is perceived as something that must be immediately eliminated, the individual will continue to seek rapid solutions. Spending, given its accessibility and effectiveness, will remain a primary option.

However, when discomfort is redefined—not as a problem to be solved, but as a state to be experienced—the urgency to act diminishes. The individual is no longer compelled to respond. They can choose.

It is important to acknowledge that this capacity develops incrementally. Initial attempts to remain present with discomfort may produce heightened awareness of emotional intensity. This is not regression; it is exposure. The individual is encountering experiences that were previously avoided, and the absence of immediate relief may feel destabilizing.

Over time, however, this exposure leads to adaptation. The individual becomes more familiar with their internal states, less reactive to fluctuations, and more capable of maintaining alignment in the presence of discomfort.

Emotional discipline, therefore, is not a passive state. It is an active process of engagement. It represents a shift from avoidance to tolerance, from reaction to response. And it is this shift that reduces the necessity of spending as a regulatory mechanism.

# Chapter 26

## Financial Honesty: Confrontation Without Distortion

Sustainable change requires accuracy. Financial honesty is the process through which that accuracy is established. It involves the direct examination of one's financial behavior without minimization, justification, or avoidance.

While awareness identifies patterns, honesty validates them. It requires the individual to move beyond partial acknowledgment and into full recognition. This includes not only what is spent, but how, when, and why it is spent. It involves confronting discrepancies between intention and action without altering the narrative to reduce discomfort.

Avoidance, in this context, is not limited to behavior. It extends to perception. Individuals may selectively address certain aspects of their financial situation while ignoring others. They may focus on income while disregarding expenditure or acknowledge isolated decisions while overlooking patterns. These distortions preserve comfort at the expense of clarity.

Financial honesty eliminates this distortion.

It requires comprehensive observation. Accounts are reviewed in their entirety. Spending is examined without selective omission. Patterns are identified across time rather than within isolated moments. The individual engages with their financial reality as it exists, not as it is preferred.

This process is not punitive. It does not involve self-criticism or moral evaluation. Its purpose is not to assign blame, but to establish an accurate baseline from which change can occur. Without this baseline, interventions lack precision. Strategies are applied without full understanding, reducing their effectiveness.

The challenge of financial honesty lies in its emotional impact. Confronting one's behavior directly may produce discomfort, particularly when patterns are well established. However, this discomfort is informative. It indicates areas of misalignment that require attention.

Through repeated engagement, the intensity of this discomfort decreases. The individual becomes accustomed to observing their financial behavior without distortion. This familiarity reduces avoidance, increasing the likelihood of sustained engagement.

Financial honesty functions as a stabilizing force. It aligns perception with reality, allowing decisions to be made from a position of clarity rather than assumption.

# Chapter 27

## The Establishment of Standards: From Temporary Goals to Consistent Identity

A critical distinction in long-term behavioral change lies between goals and standards. Goals are temporal; they are pursued, achieved, or abandoned. Standards, by contrast, are continuous. They define the way an individual operates regardless of circumstance.

Emotional spending often persists in environments governed by goals rather than standards. The individual sets intentions—reduce spending, save more, adhere to a budget—but these intentions are contingent upon motivation. When motivation fluctuates, adherence declines.

Standards eliminate this variability.

A standard is not something one attempts; it is something one maintains. It is integrated into identity and expressed through consistent behavior. Statements such as "I do not make emotional purchases" or "I pause before spending" are not aspirational; they are declarative. They define how decisions are made.

The adoption of standards simplifies decision-making. Rather than evaluating each situation independently, the individual operates within predefined parameters. This reduces cognitive load and limits the influence of fluctuating emotional states.

Importantly, standards are not rigid to the point of inflexibility. They allow for context, but they do not permit contradiction. The individual may adapt their behavior within the framework of the standard, but they do not abandon the framework itself.

The transition from goals to standards represents a shift in orientation. The individual is no longer attempting to change behavior intermittently; they are redefining how behavior is expressed consistently. This shift is foundational to identity integration.

Over time, adherence to standards produces cumulative effects. Behavior becomes predictable, self-trust is reinforced, and the individual's perception of themselves evolves. They no longer view alignment as an effortful act, but as a default mode of operation.

# Chapter 28

## Eliminating the Need for Escape: Reconstructing Internal Stability

At its core, emotional spending is an attempt to escape. It provides temporary distance from discomfort, offering relief without resolution. To reduce reliance on this mechanism, the individual must develop an alternative: the capacity to remain within their experience without seeking immediate exit.

This does not imply that discomfort is desirable or that it should be prolonged unnecessarily. Rather, it acknowledges that avoidance, while effective in the short term, perpetuates the conditions that produce the need for escape.

Internal stability is achieved through engagement, not avoidance.

When individuals develop the capacity to process their experiences directly, whether through reflection, regulation, or deliberate action, the intensity of those experiences diminishes. They are no longer perceived as overwhelming and therefore do not necessitate immediate resolution.

As this capacity increases, the perceived necessity of spending decreases. The individual no longer relies on external mechanisms to manage internal states. Relief is no longer contingent upon acquisition; it is generated through engagement.

This shift has profound implications. It alters the individual's relationship with both emotion and behavior. Discomfort becomes manageable, rather than threatening. Decisions are made in alignment with long-term objectives, rather than immediate needs.

The elimination of the need for escape does not occur instantaneously. It is the result of repeated exposure to discomfort without avoidance, coupled with the development of effective regulatory strategies. Over time, the individual's baseline level of stability increases, reducing the frequency and intensity of reactive behaviors.

In this state, spending is no longer a coping mechanism. It becomes what it was intended to be: a functional, deliberate act.

# Chapter 29

## Forward Continuity: Progress Without Regression to "Starting Over"

A common misconception in behavioral change is the notion of "starting over." Individuals interpret deviations from intended behavior as resets, discarding prior progress and reinitiating the process from an assumed baseline. This interpretation is both inaccurate and counterproductive.

Change is not linear, but it is cumulative.

Each instance of awareness, interruption, and aligned behavior contributes to the overall pattern. Deviations do not negate this accumulation; they provide additional data. The individual is not returning to a prior state but continuing from an expanded level of understanding.

The concept of forward continuity reframes setbacks. Rather than viewing them as failures, they are interpreted as extensions of the learning process. The individual examines the conditions under which the deviation occurred, identifies contributing factors, and integrates this information into future behavior.

This approach reduces the likelihood of disengagement. When setbacks are perceived as evidence of failure, individuals may abandon efforts entirely. In contrast, when they are understood as part of an ongoing process, persistence is maintained.

Forward continuity also reinforces self-trust. The individual recognizes that their capacity for alignment is not eliminated by occasional inconsistency. They retain confidence in their ability to return to established patterns, reducing the emotional impact of deviations.

## Part VI Closing Insight

The culmination of this process is not merely behavioral change, but identity integration. The individual transitions from reacting to emotional states through spending to engaging with those states directly. They develop systems that support alignment, standards that define behavior, and the capacity to maintain consistency in the presence of discomfort.

This transformation is not characterized by perfection. It is characterized by stability.

Spending no longer functions as an escape mechanism. It is decoupled from emotional regulation and redefined as a deliberate, controlled action. The individual no longer relies on external acquisition to manage internal experience.

Instead, they operate from a position of awareness, discipline, and self-trust.

And in that position, the pattern that once dominated their behavior loses its relevance—not because it has been forcibly eliminated, but because it is no longer necessary.

# CONCLUSION

## From Awareness to Alignment

At this stage, the objective is no longer comprehension. The framework has been established, the behavioral mechanisms examined, and the systems for change clearly outlined. What remains is execution—specifically, the integration of understanding into consistent behavior.

Throughout this work, emotional spending has been reframed as a patterned response rather than a financial deficiency. This distinction is not semantic; it is operational. It shifts the point of intervention from isolated financial decisions to the underlying processes that produce them.

Patterns do not dissolve through intention alone. They persist until they are recognized, interrupted, and replaced.

What has changed is not the existence of the pattern, but your visibility of it.

You now understand the sequence: the emotional trigger, the internal justification, the impulse, and the anticipated relief. You can identify the moment in which a decision begins to form. That moment, previously unnoticed, is now accessible.

And access changes everything.

Because behavior that is visible can be influenced. Behavior that is understood can be redirected. Behavior that is repeatedly redirected can be replaced.

This is the transition from awareness to alignment.

Alignment is not achieved through intensity. It is achieved through consistency. It is the repeated act of making decisions that reflect what you already know to be true. Not occasionally. Not when it is convenient. But consistently enough that it becomes your default.

This process is not immediate. It is cumulative.

Each decision you make from awareness strengthens the new pattern. Each pause, each boundary, each refusal to act on impulse contributes to a shift that is gradual but definitive. Over time, what once required effort becomes automatic.

This is not the elimination of desire. It is the removal of its control.

You will still experience stress, boredom, comparison, and emotional fluctuation. The difference is that these states will no longer dictate your behavior. They will exist without requiring a financial response.

That is stability.

Not the absence of emotion, but the absence of reactivity.

## The Point of No Return

There is a moment in every behavioral shift where awareness reaches a threshold. Beyond this threshold, previous interpretations are no longer sustainable.

You have reached that point.

Prior to this, it was possible to attribute financial behavior to circumstance, oversight, or incomplete understanding. Now, those explanations no longer hold. The pattern has been identified in full. Its structure is clear. Its consequences are understood.

This does not make change easier.

It makes avoidance more difficult.

You now recognize when you are responding to discomfort rather than acting intentionally. You hear the internal narratives that attempt to justify misalignment. You see the long-term trade-offs behind short-term decisions.

This awareness does not remove choice. It clarifies it.

And clarified choice introduces responsibility—not as a burden, but as a capability. You are now equipped to respond differently. Whether you do so consistently is determined not by knowledge, but by application.

## The Observing Self

As this awareness stabilizes, a distinct shift occurs in how you experience your own behavior.

You begin to observe yourself in real time.

This is not a new ability, but a strengthened one. It may have appeared previously as hesitation, second-guessing, or a brief recognition that a decision was misaligned. Now, it becomes consistent.

You notice the impulse as it arises. You recognize the justification before it completes. You are aware of the moment in which a decision could go in either direction.

This is the observing self.

Its function is not to judge or control. Its function is to reveal.

And once revealed, behavior is no longer automatic.

This is where agency develops—not in the absence of impulse, but in the presence of awareness. The observing self creates the space in which a different response becomes possible.

The more it is engaged, the more influential it becomes.

## Continuity, Not Restart

A critical error in behavioral change is the belief that deviation requires restart.

It does not.

Change is not a sequence of perfect actions. It is a pattern of increasing alignment. Deviation is not the opposite of progress; it is part of it. It provides information about conditions, triggers, and gaps in the current system.

The distinction lies in response.

If deviation leads to disengagement, the pattern remains unchanged. If deviation leads to analysis and adjustment, the pattern evolves.

You are not starting over.

You are continuing with more information than you had before.

This continuity preserves progress. It prevents the cycle of abandonment and reinitiation that characterizes unsustainable change. It allows you to remain within the process, even when consistency fluctuates.

## Standards as Structure

Motivation is inherently unstable. It fluctuates with mood, environment, and circumstance. As such, it cannot serve as the foundation for consistent behavior.

Standards provide that foundation.

A standard is a predefined way of operating that does not require negotiation in the moment. It removes ambiguity. It simplifies decision-making. It establishes consistency independent of emotional state.

When you operate from standards, decisions are no longer evaluated based on how you feel. They are evaluated based on whether they align.

This reduces internal conflict.

Over time, standards become integrated into identity. They are no longer experienced as restrictions, but as expressions of how you function. The effort required to maintain them decreases as repetition increases.

## Self-Respect as Action

Self-respect, within this framework, is not an abstract concept. It is behavioral.

It is the consistent alignment between what you intend and what you do.

It is expressed in decisions that are often unremarkable: pausing before acting, honoring a boundary, choosing not to engage in a familiar pattern. These decisions are not visible to others. They do not produce immediate recognition.

Their significance lies in accumulation.

Each aligned action reinforces internal credibility. Over time, this credibility becomes self-trust. You begin to rely on your own decisions because you have evidence that you follow through.

This is how identity changes.

Not through declaration, but through repeated demonstration.

## Final Integration

The objective of this work was not to eliminate spending, but to remove its role as an emotional coping mechanism.

That objective is achieved not through restriction, but through replacement.

You have developed awareness of your patterns. You have learned to interrupt them. You have introduced alternative responses. You have established boundaries and standards. You have begun to separate behavior from identity.

These elements, when applied consistently, create a new system.

Within that system, spending is no longer automatic. It is deliberate.

It no longer functions as escape. It functions as choice.

And once spending is no longer required to regulate emotion, its influence diminishes.

Not because it has been removed, but because it is no longer necessary.

# FINAL ESSENCE TRUTH

You did not lack discipline.
You lacked visibility.

You did not lack control.
You were operating within a system you had not yet examined.

Now you have.

And from this point forward—
you are not reacting.

You are choosing.

# MY FINANCIAL TRUTH

This section establishes your baseline. It is not reflective in a general sense. It is specific, detailed, and complete.

Document your current financial position without omission.

Record your total debt as it exists. Do not estimate. Do not round. Precision is required.

Identify purchases that were concealed, minimized, or justified. These are not isolated incidents; they are indicators of pattern.

List all financial accounts, including those not consistently reviewed or acknowledged. Transparency is essential.

Examine recurring expenses. Subscriptions, automatic payments, and habitual spending must be identified and evaluated. Patterns often exist in repetition, not in single transactions.

Acknowledge instances in which money was allocated under one premise and used for another. These discrepancies provide insight into behavioral inconsistency.

From this information, identify recurring patterns. These patterns should be described clearly and without generalization.

Finally, define the changes you will implement. These must be specific and aligned with the systems outlined in this work. General intentions are insufficient.

This is your point of reference.

Without an accurate baseline, change cannot be measured or sustained.

# 30-DAY FINANCIAL INTEGRITY RESET

This is a structured recalibration process. It is not designed to produce immediate results, but to establish consistent behavioral patterns.

## Week 1: Observational Awareness

All financial activity is recorded in real time. No estimation. No omission.

Daily account review is required. Avoidance is not permitted.

At the end of the week, identify patterns without evaluating them.

## Week 2: Behavioral Transparency

All spending is acknowledged now it occurs.

Internal justifications are documented and examined.

There is no separation between action and awareness.

### Week 3: Structured Intervention

Implement predefined spending boundaries.

Apply a pause to all non-essential purchases.

Introduce and evaluate alternative behaviors for emotional regulation.

### Week 4: Pattern Stabilization

Repeat aligned behaviors consistently.

Evaluate progress based on adherence, not outcomes.

Analyze deviations and adjust systems accordingly.

# Final Back Matter Insight

Change is not produced through intention alone.

It occurs when patterns are consistently interrupted and replaced with behaviors that align with long-term outcomes.

This process marks the transition from unconscious reaction to deliberate action.

From this point forward, your behavior is no longer incidental.

It is intentional.

www.ingramcontent.com/pod-product-compliance
Lightning Source LLC
LaVergne TN
LVHW010625100826
845148LV00014B/3107